BRITISH AND AMERICAN PLAYWRIGHTS
1750–1920

General editors: Martin Banham and Peter Thomson

George Colman the Younger and Thomas Morton

OTHER VOLUMES IN THIS SERIES

Already published:

TOM ROBERTSON edited by William Tydeman
W.S. GILBERT edited by George Rowell
HENRY ARTHUR JONES edited by Russell Jackson
DAVID GARRICK AND GEORGE COLMAN THE ELDER edited by E.R. Wood
WILLIAM GILLETTE edited by Don Wilmeth and Rosemary Cullen

Further volumes will include:

J.R. PLANCHÉ edited by Don Roy
A.W. PINERO edited by Martin Banham
DION BOUCICAULT edited by Peter Thomson
CHARLES READE edited by M. Hammet
TOM TAYLOR edited by Martin Banham
ARTHUR MURPHY AND SAMUEL FOOTE edited by George Taylor
H.J. BYRON edited by J.T.L. Davis
AUGUSTIN DALY edited by Don Wilmeth and Rosemary Cullen